During my time [...] I had the privileg[e ...] le Lamont Lester. [...] ly how deeply he cares about our youth, but just how gifted he is at connecting with them. He has a way of quickly earning their trust and utilizes that trust to engage, encourage, and inspire. Along with the ability for connecting with kids, Lamont continually demonstrates incredible leadership qualities that motivate staff, volunteers, and community members to want to do more in support of our youth and teens. While Lamont's impact is vast, it also runs deep which is vital in shaping how to best serve each individual. He is an inspiration to me and I'm proud to call him my friend.

Steve Saxton
District Executive Director
YMCA of Middle Tennessee

Lamont demonstrates a true heart for children. His leadership, experience, and expertise give him the ability to connect to youth in a way that builds trust and encourages communication. Trust and communication are key steppingstones towards healthy adults.

Zannie Martin
Director Juvenile Court
Williamson County TN

"Lamont Lester has been helping people "find their way" for a very long time. In "The Language of Life" he has integrated the wisdom that has come from all those years of experience. In this book he lays the groundwork for an exciting new approach to counseling he calls "map therapy." This book provides an innovative language and a fresh way of imagining precisely where you are in life and how to get to where you feel called to go."

Michael Card
American singer-songwriter, musician, and author

Lamont Lester is a beacon of light and hope for the young people in our community. He sees the best in our youth and always finds the right avenues to expose their hearts and voices. He has a beautiful story of his own, one of restoration, promise, and empowerment.

Josiah Holland
School Administrator
Director
Alternative Learning Center
Williamson County Schools

L.O.L.
THE LANGUAGE OF LIFE

Learning to Laugh Along the Journey

LAMONT LESTER

WESTBOW
PRESS®
A DIVISION OF THOMAS NELSON
& ZONDERVAN

Copyright © 2021 Lamont Lester.

All rights reserved. No part of this book may be used or reproduced by any means, graphic, electronic, or mechanical, including photocopying, recording, taping or by any information storage retrieval system without the written permission of the author except in the case of brief quotations embodied in critical articles and reviews.

This book is a work of non-fiction. Unless otherwise noted, the author and the publisher make no explicit guarantees as to the accuracy of the information contained in this book and in some cases, names of people and places have been altered to protect their privacy.

WestBow Press books may be ordered through booksellers or by contacting:

WestBow Press
A Division of Thomas Nelson & Zondervan
1663 Liberty Drive
Bloomington, IN 47403
www.westbowpress.com
844-714-3454

Because of the dynamic nature of the Internet, any web addresses or links contained in this book may have changed since publication and may no longer be valid. The views expressed in this work are solely those of the author and do not necessarily reflect the views of the publisher, and the publisher hereby disclaims any responsibility for them.

Any people depicted in stock imagery provided by Getty Images are models, and such images are being used for illustrative purposes only. Certain stock imagery © Getty Images.

Scripture taken from the King James Version of the Bible.

ISBN: 978-1-6642-4209-8 (sc)
ISBN: 978-1-6642-4210-4 (hc)
ISBN: 978-1-6642-4208-1 (e)

Library of Congress Control Number: 2021915932

Print information available on the last page.

WestBow Press rev. date: 08/26/2021

TO MY DAD

My father George W. Lester Jr. has been my biggest cheerleader from day one. The reason I wanted to dedicate this is because he's not only that for me but has been for his entire family for as long as I can remember. George Jr., as many call him, should be rewarded for his tireless labor of love he continues to give to his wife, his children, and his grandchildren. Each of know that we can call on him for anything, and if he's able to do it he will. That says a lot when we're dealing with the most fatherless generation we've had in America. I think it also says a lot because there are several men that have no idea where their kids are or what they are doing. George Jr. keeps a close ear to the needs of all that belong to him, and I wanted to take this time to salute him and share with the world, that there is one doing it well and his name is George Wallace Lester Jr. I love you dad! Thank you for being you.

TO MY GIRL

This page goes to my "Purpose Partner", Lovie Lester! You totally deserve a page for taming this old lion. Lol. Lovie you are the best thing that has happened to me since Jesus Christ, and I thank you for your continued patience and unconditional love that you have shown me over the years. We have been through so much together and seen the hand of the Lord move mountains in our lives. It has been an incredible ride and I can truly say that there is no one that I could have enjoyed this journey more with, than you. This life that we have built together is the more than I could have ever imagined. You were strong enough to endure the struggles of a young man with a vision, while he found his way through the wilderness looking for a "Promised Land". We haven't found it yet, but I can sure say that it's a beautiful road that we're on leading up to it. Thank you for being exactly what I needed to assist me in everyway that has been needed over these last 20+ years. I'm convinced that we're on the right track and that our latter shall be greater! Thank you for partnering with me on this journey young lady. Now go ahead and tighten your seatbelt and enjoy the ride because we're really just getting started. Love you girl!

FOREWORD

What if I told you, you speak another language, and you probably don't even know that you do? What if I told you that language you don't know you know consisted of a vocabulary that helps you articulate where you've been, where you are, and where you want to go? What if I told you that language could be integrated onto a map, a chart that plotted the positions of your past, present, and future?

Welcome to Map Language Therapy (MLT), a new approach to understanding your life as a journey on your own personal map.

The basic concept is almost as old as language itself. The fundamental principles of Map Language Therapy are rooted in our everyday speech. It is a part of the way we think about life. We speak of being stuck on a "dead-end street." We say we are "lost" or it will be a "long road" to recovery. We already use language to place ourselves on an imaginary map. What if we could learn to chart our position on the map of our lives and gain an understanding of where we have been and where we are, and chart a course for where we want to go? What if we could visualize, name, and give shape to the basic elements of the different pathways of an individual life? This is Map Language Therapy.

Once you understand the basics, there are myriad applications of this technique. You might begin by charting your own personal cartography or try mapping the lives of your favorite biblical characters. MLT could even help you plot the course of your marriage: where it has been, where it might have taken a wrong turn, and the direction you want it to go.

So welcome once again to the adventure we call Map Language Therapy.

PART 1

CHAPTER 1

UNAPOLOGETIC

Life is a journey. On this journey, you will experience highs and lows and everything in between. These experiences will also give you lenses to see through that will affect every decision you face. These lenses are created by your perception of what is good and what is evil. Based on your experiences, your life lenses will give you a language. This book offers a new language to help you translate your life experiences and get you to your desired place in life—that place called purpose.

On October 31, 1969, I was born to George and Lillie Lester in Nashville, Tennessee. While I was your typical child, I soon realized that few of the people in my neighborhood and family had their dad living in the home. Several family members and most of my friends grew up without their fathers living with them. As I've gotten older, the importance of having a supportive father in the home has become more apparent. My parents were the perfect balance of wrath and grace when it came to raising my younger sister and me. If you know anything about the way I grew up, it is evident who brought the wrath. However, both were very supportive, and they have been married over fifty years. Thankfully, we were able to celebrate them both as each turned eighty years old.

When I turned fifty last year, it was very significant. There have been many times in my life when I thought I would never see that happen. There are also many who felt the same way. I remember stretches in my life when I heard people say, "You're going to end up dead or in prison." I remember years when my mom refused to answer the phone at night because she thought someone was calling to tell her something happened to me. Looking back, I know it was nothing but the grace of God that kept me here, and I am extremely grateful.

Thankfully, God continues to prove me and my critics all wrong because I ended up okay. My experiences allow me to assist others and help them through the difficult times they are experiencing. That's the real reason I wrote this book. Those fifty years of lessons have brought me to the place where I now help boys, men, families, leaders, and churches solve critical issues. Trust me—only God could have done this. In a day where discipleship and mentors are so needed, there seems to be few people who want to take on that mantle. Sadly, many have embraced the "every man for himself" attitude. Is it possible that COVID-19 and the spotlight on social justice have returned our attention to valuing people, our family members, neighbors, and friends? I think it could be. That is just my two cents.

Now back to the subject at hand. You can most likely discern that I am big on discipleship and mentoring. I have been called a mentoring guru. If you want to grow and develop to a level of maturity in any area of life, discipleship and mentoring are key. We all need a model to emulate. Now, there have been times when I took my God-given gift of leadership and used it to send people down the wrong path. I have been the villain and the hero, depending on the season.

You see, you are not reading a book from a person who did everything right. Nor are you reading a book from a person who has it all together and does not make mistakes. You are reading a book written by someone who has messed up many times and will mess up again. I am extremely flawed. As a matter of fact, I might be messing up while you are reading this book, but that's okay. I am good at messing up. I think it has become my learning style: messing up, learning from it, owning my mistakes, and doing it differently next time around. In a society where people are okay being so fake, I think it is refreshing to see true authenticity and transparency. I have learned to love and embrace the fact that I have always been honest and real. Phony people are kept at bay. Now I must admit that my level of keeping it real has gotten me in a few messes, but the grace of God has been sufficient and continues to keep me safe.

Disclaimer: This book shows you the real, authentic, transparent, and honest Lamont Lester. I personally feel my honesty allows me to connect with people from all walks of life. What you see is what you get: good, bad, and ugly. Now, for the record, I am saved and love Jesus with all my heart, my soul, and my mind. Please do not get that twisted. I also think I have a pretty good sense of humor, so be prepared for anything. I got that from my mama, the one and only Ms. Lilly. She has always been hilarious. Consequently, humor has become a part of my DNA. My wife also has a cool sense of humor, which we have passed on to our kids, Sam and Marlena. The Bible speaks of laughter being good medicine, and we take our doses every day. We make jokes and really enjoy life.

To understand me a little better, I was raised by old-school parents who did not sugarcoat what they said. In this book, I am going to give it to you like I got it, so don't be alarmed by what you read. Revelation 12:11 talks about the word of their testimony. This book is simply me sharing my testimony in a way that will give you tools to share and articulate your journey so you can help others overcome obstacles and walk freely in their own destinies. As you read it, you will begin to pick up a reoccurring theme and start to put the pieces together for your own story.

This book is broken down into two parts. The first part is my own personal journey, shared in a unique way that will allow you to learn a new language and map out your own story. This language will make some of the things you have been through digestible so you can free yourself and others. After you read my story, you will be aware of obstacles and forces that are out there trying to keep you from your destiny.

The second part consists of a concept that I used to tell my story, that you can make your own. There are instructions and a language to assist you in developing and designing your own journey, which you will use to share your story. Your story will allow you to help people by assisting them in their journey, using areas you have successfully worked through.

Before we get started, I do want to thank you for choosing to read this book. It has taken me many years to get comfortable with who God made me to be. In today's world, we have been mistakenly taught that we need to live up to a certain standard to be considered significant or, in current terms, essential. I strived for years to reach human-made expectations for me; it's been exhausting and unobtainable. However, settling into who God says I am has been the most fulfilling experience I have had. It is a life that keeps giving and giving and giving. With that being said, I pray that this book ignites something in you that allows you to walk in your full authenticity and celebrate who God created you to be through your experiences.

❓ REFLECTION QUESTIONS

How do you view yourself?

Do you feel that you are significant or essential?

Do you see your authenticity as a blessing or a curse?

Do you feel that you have a purpose or have been put on earth for a reason?

What do you bring to the world?

CHAPTER 2

IN WALKS THE LION

Over the years, I have found myself reading scripture and applying it to help me stay on the right course. One of the first scriptures I remember is 1 Peter 5:8, NIV: "Be alert and of sober mind. Your enemy the devil prowls around like a roaring lion looking for someone to devour." I thought this scripture was scary when I first decided to give my life to Christ. I took some time to reflect and ask, "When did I encounter my first lion?" I believe when we are born, God has a plan for our lives. I also believe that the devil is a real force who desires to get us away from the path God has laid out for us. Unfortunately, the devil uses people to do his dirty work.

I ran into my first lion in the fifth grade. It came in the form of a bully who shall remain nameless. This bully was older than most of the kids; he had gotten left a couple of times. Imagine that. He was like Debo in the movie *Friday*, but this was elementary school. He always took kids' lunch money and approached me on a couple of occasions. I was scared and ended up telling my father about the situation. The next day, my dad went up to Glendale Elementary and met with the principal. The bullying ended that day. I was teased a little later for telling, but I was just glad that the bullying was over. Ironically, I now work with kids who experience bullying and all other types of mental and physical abuse.

Two years later, I was in the seventh grade at John Trotwood Moore Middle School, and I had another run-in with bullies. This new bully was huge and played on the football team. My best friend and I used to hide in the lockers during break because a couple of guys would terrorize kids. One day, my friend and I went different ways, and one of the bullies caught me before I could get into my hiding place. Of course, he started messing with me. At that point, he had caught me on a day where I think I had had enough.

He pushed me, and I pushed him back. He pushed me again, as the crowd egged him on, and I pushed back again.

He said, "Aw, you bad today?"

I just said that I wasn't for it.

He said, "Well, I am going to whoop your tail," and I responded, "Not today."

I was terrified but too far out there to turn back. The next thing I knew, the whole school was following us to the boy's restroom to watch us fight. We went inside, with everyone following in anticipation. He swung and punched me. After that, I just remember whaling and swinging.

I continued until he said, "Hold up, hold up."

I stopped and said, "What's up?"

He said, "We good."

I said, "Don't hit me."

He said, "I just wanted to see where your heart was at, Lester."

Imagine that? I knew that was not the case. He simply had no idea how to stop that flurry of blows; they came out of nowhere. I didn't even know where they came from.

We shook hands, and that was the last time I got bullied. Come to find out, he was recovering from a football injury, where he had broken his nose. What he also didn't know was that my dad used to box and had showed me a few things over the years. I also had a few little fights in the neighborhood, along with several boxing matches with cousins and friends. But I had never gotten into a real fight, with people watching and egging it on. That is probably another reason I work with young people. Take my little story and add the internet and social media to it. Now you have cyber bullying and people from across town instigating and pulling strings. That is a lot for our young people to contend with today. That one fight changed my life and set me on a course that would haunt me for years to come. Some roads this life puts you on are very complicated, and sometimes, it's nearly impossible to get off.

That was just one example of many lions I have come across. We know offenses will come, but how we respond determines how we see ourselves and others as we navigate through this thing called life.

Now, what do you do when the lion is in your family? What if you are married to the lion? What if the lion is an abuser or molester? Right now, during the pandemic, reports of domestic, child, and sexual abuse are down, but many people are being forced to quarantine with their abusers. Depression, suicide, and substance abuse are on the rise, as people try to get through the pandemic. Not to mention the #MeToo Movement that came to the forefront a couple of years ago. Women from all walks of life began to come out and share that they had been violated by lions but never told anyone.

In the black community, we are told, "Don't speak out of my house." The truth of the matter is, there are people of all ages, from all walks of life, who have been knocked off their course because the devil used someone to do something, and now they are suffering in silence. It is not their fault. There is a real enemy (a lion) who wants to devour you. It is the devil.

Unfortunately, I have worked with youth where family members, a stepparent, or family friend violated them and caused trauma in ways you cannot imagine. These offenses may never be confronted, and the victim has to live through all the trauma that comes with the hurt, while still trying to get their lives back on course.

⁇ REFLECTION QUESTIONS

What do you do when life knocks you off course through the actions of someone else?

What was the first lion you remember encountering?

Did you ever confront the lion?

Has someone or something taken you off your course?

How have you gotten back on the right course?

CHAPTER 3

WHAT FRUIT ARE YOU BEARING?

With this newly developed skill set, I found myself getting into fights all the time and became known as a fighter and troublemaker. Now I become a lion. Imagine that. I ended up starting a gang in South Nashville, which became a force to be reckoned with. We were thick as thieves and didn't take anything from anyone. We even had our own language. Someone would page me (there were no cell phones back then) and say, "Les, we have a discrepancy." That meant someone was going to get beat down. "Les" and "Les Chill" were my street tags. I am still friends with many of the guys who survived. I say "survived" because many of us served time for drugs or robbery, have been in and out of rehabilitation facilities, and even murdered people. I do not to speak ill toward my friends because I was one of them, at that time in my life. However, when we get together now, we thank God we made it to the other side. Most of us are now hardworking men with families who make a positive impact on our community.

Over the past couple of years, I have been working in Williamson County Schools, Juvenile Court and the Williamson County Alternative Learning Center. I present workshops to young people that deal with everything from drugs, conflict resolution, anger management, and life skills to decision making. I really enjoy working with young men because I share with them that, "I was like you, but will you be like me?" I've done about 90 percent of everything they have done, and I'm still here to talk about it. The question is, will they be able to do these things and make it to the age of fifty and be able to tell others how they made it?

These young men often say, "Mr. Lamont, I'm not the thing I continue to get in trouble for." At that time, I usually share with them that their actions may place them in a specific category. The book of Matthew says that you can tell a tree by its fruit.

All of this brings me to a stretch in my life where I allowed peer pressure and bad decisions to dictate who I was perceived to be. Because I was always fighting and starting trouble, I was called a thug, troublemaker, dope dealer, hoodlum, and so on. I was often suspended from school, kicked out of events, and labeled for some of the choices of my youth, even after I stopped making those choices. That's why I can relate to these young men. Bad choices put you on a path I call Shame Street. This is where you make a bad choice and end up regretting what you did and reflecting on where you went wrong. I personally have traveled many miles on this unpopular road.

I share all of this because you will begin to see a pattern and language that you will be able to use for yourself. For example, let me tell you about Shame Street. I believe we have all done things we are ashamed of. I know I have, but there is a distinct difference between private and public shame. Shame Street is where you end up when everyone knows you messed up. When I say everyone, it is usually people you tried to pull the wool over their eyes so they think you are really good, like your family, church members, teachers, and so on.

Let me tell you about Shame Street. By the time I was a senior in high school, I had a reputation for several things, none of them good. As I shared earlier, I think I have a pretty good sense of humor, and I also became a class clown. As you know, this title is not a good one, and unfortunately, it makes you always want to one-up someone for a laugh.

Imagine me in my senior year at John Overton High School in 1987, getting ready to graduate. In order to graduate, I had to take a biology class. We were studying animals and learned how to dissect them. With my warped sense of humor, I thought it would be funny to take one of the frogs and scare people with it. So of course, I did. I chased a couple of girls down the hall for laughs. You might think that would have been enough, but no; I had to do more. That is what peer pressure and trying to impress people will do, unfortunately.

My next class was called Commercial Foods. This is where you learn to cook, and we had the coolest teacher, named Mr. Pagan. Everybody loved Mr. Pagan. As class was about to begin, I got this bright idea and shared it with my good friend, Anthony Abernathy (RIP). I told Anthony I was going to chop the frog up and put it in the food in the cafeteria.

Anthony laughed and said, "No, you aren't."

I said, "Yes, I am."

So instead of me going to class like everyone else, I snuck into the kitchen, grabbed a sandwich bag and a knife, and start chopping this frog up.

It just so happens that Commercial Foods was the first class to eat lunch, and that day, there was a self-serve taco bar. So now gassed up, I let my friends go first and then went behind them. I pulled the frog out of my pocket, took the pieces, and stirred them deep into the taco meat. Anthony and the rest of my crew went to a table and just sat in anticipation. Wait for it: About five minutes later, a girl jumped from her table, screaming. She had dug up a frog leg, and it was sitting on top of her taco meat. We screamed. We were all on the floor with tears in our eyes, hysterical.

It was awesome, until I heard over the intercom, "Lamont Lester, come to the office."

I sobered up quickly, and it was not funny anymore. Imagine that?

I started trying to get my lies together before I got the office to see the principal (who, by the way, hated me, and in hindsight, I understand why). He asked me about the frog, and of course, I lied. I lied, lied, and lied again.

Now in 1987, no one was used to dealing with terrorist acts, but I learned that day. The principal told me he could not handle me, so he would call in the Health Department and let them know I tried to poison the whole school. They would deal with it as a terrorist act.

My next words were, "I did it." I did not know what would happen, but I had enough sense to know I didn't want to get things turned over into anyone's hands outside of the school system.

This foolish act put me on Shame Street. I was suspended; they kicked me out of school for the rest of the year, and I did not graduate. I had to repeat my entire senior year. In the long run, it was not funny. It was humiliating. My parents were pillars in the community, and my mother was an educator who had helped kids from all over the city, and now her son was the one acting a fool.

I have run into a few people over the years, and when they see me, they bust out laughing and say, "Lamont, you remember when you put that frog in the taco salad?"

I just change the subject. Trust me, on this side, it is shameful, and I truly regret that bad decision.

That was not the last time I hung out on Shame Street. One thing that happens to most of us is, as we grow out of making bad decisions, we feel that we let God down. After giving my life to Christ, I remember the pressure of feeling that you had to do everything right, and if you did not, you would feel convicted. There were also times in my Christian walk that I have done what is called backsliding.

Those public mistakes can put you on Shame Street as well. Sometimes, when Christians know you messed up, they won't let you off Shame Street. We will talk about that later. I share this so it helps you to understand Shame Street so that maybe when you share your story, it can set someone else free.

⸮‽⸮ REFLECTION QUESTIONS

Can you recall when you had to take a walk down Shame Street?

What bad decisions have you made that altered your course?

How would you encourage others to overcome their shame?

Are you on Shame Street today?

CHAPTER 4

LAMONT MEETS BROKENNESS

I GUESS YOU PROBABLY WOULD HAVE THOUGHT THAT two senior years would have helped me get on the right track, but it did not. I played a while on Fool's Hill (for this book's sake, let's call it Rebellion Ridge). Later on, I discuss the many hills and valleys in life, where people get caught up in all types of uncomfortable situations. Rebellion Ridge has traps that are designed to get you off your course and, in some cases, kill you. You can get lost in them there hills. There are all types of stories of people who have been seriously injured. Sadly, some never make it to the other side.

I ended up going to college but never applied myself. During those years of rebellion, I found myself involved in everything, including selling and using drugs. I'm not proud of those years because I dabbled in a little bit of everything, trying to find my way. The one thing I did have going for me was a good work ethic. I had gotten that from my parents, who had always strived to improve our lives.

When I was about twenty-three, I settled into the fact that I blew college and wasn't going back to school. I got a job at Target and stayed there about six years, working my way up.

This was when I began to recognize that customer service and working with people was something I liked and excelled at. I decided to work on the overnight shift because you could make a dollar more, and I could free up my days. My father had always worked overnight and seemed to like it, so I gave it a shot. At this point, I was doing pretty good for myself and was in my seventh year at Target. On the overnight shift, we would joke all the time.

I was good at joking on people out of necessity. I grew up at a time when being dark skinned was not popular. Unfortunately, in the black community, we sometimes hurt each other with our words. I tell people today that there is nothing a white person can say to me that is worse than what my own people have said. I work with youth and know countless people who have had their self-esteem crushed by the words that have come from African Americans under the premise of joking. Luckily for me, all of that changed right around eighth grade, when Michael Jordan and Wesley Snipes came on the scene. Dark skin was in, and I went from the bottom to the top. Thank you, Jesus. The Bible says the last shall be first, and now dark skin is on top. That is a joke, but now I guess we need to get back on track.

As I was saying, I became pretty good and could verbally assault a person with the greatest of ease. My mouth generally got me into trouble and a lot of fights. That is exactly what happened at Target. I got into this joking match with someone at work and verbally destroyed them. They picked up a chair, called me a racial slur, and then tried to hit me with it. They missed and paid a dear price for swinging a chair at me. Of course, we both got fired, and now I was completely out of options. I had messed up a job that I liked.

This new bad decision put me right back on Shame Street. As I was going back and forth verbally, I passed Escape Parkway and Self-Control Boulevard. Either of these roads could have changed my whole trajectory, but I drove right past them. I hope you are beginning to see the pattern. The Bible says that with every temptation, there is a way of escape. I could have defused the situation or even practiced self-control and walked away, but I did not. Once again, I had allowed my pride and my anger take over and put me right back on Shame Street. I lost a good job, and after all those years, I could not even use them as a reference.

At this point, I began to reflect on all the fun I thought I was having on Rebellion Ridge, with true regret. I started looking at myself, my decisions, and my life. I remember looking in the newspaper every day for a job. At that time, the only place that I could get hired was a downtown parking lot attendant. They hired me for $4.05 an hour. I was devastated. I had gone from making around $13 to $4.05. This was when I hung out in the Brokenness District. I would sit in my booth, handing parking tickets out the window, with a want ad and my Bible. I would look for jobs and read the Word every day. This was also the place where most people make the "brokenness promise": "God, if you get me out of this, I promise …" I followed suit. I found out that even if you end up on Shame Street, keep moving and praying. God has a way of getting you back on track.

One day, while doing my daily routine of checking the want ads and reading the Bible, I ran across an opening at Eycom Gulf Industries Inc. It said that I could make up to fifteen hundred dollars a week and travel all over the country, selling outdoor and indoor lighting signs to independent business owners. It was a cold-call, straight commission, one call close job. It was the hardest thing I had ever done in my life up to that point.

I took the job and hit the road the following week. My manager's name was Bill, who I consider one of the angels the Lord put in my path. Angels are people God puts in your life to help you get back on course.

Bill was one of the best salesmen in the world. He took me under his wing and made me read books on the road, books by Og Mandingo, Tom Hopkins, and Zig Ziglar. He made me listen to tapes and learn the art of selling. Once again, I excelled at this newly discovered ability. I was able to take my street hustle and mix it in with my new professional trade to relate to anyone. Bill's heavy hand in making me learn how to become a great salesman continues to pay dividends in my life till this day. This job also got me out of South Nashville and away from old friends and mindsets that had kept me bound for years. I was now able to see the world through a totally different set of lenses, which changed me forever.

Visiting the Broken District allowed God to humble me; I depended on Him to restore me and get me on the right track. I have been there a few times. Next, I'll introduce you to my whole neighborhood.

❓ REFLECTION QUESTIONS

Have you ever been broken?

Who helped you get back on course?

Did you view your place of brokenness as good or bad?

Has brokenness ever worked for the good in your life?

CHAPTER 5

FINALLY ON THE RIGHT COURSE

When I was on the road as a traveling salesman, I really began to develop my relationship with the Lord. I kept praying for traveling mercies because I did not want to have an accident or get hurt while out of town. I also worked on straight commissions. That increased my faith and prayer life. Four years later, as my relationship with the Lord grew, I got to a point where I was tired of traveling and wanted to be able to serve in a local church and be a part of ministry.

I decided to come off the road and started going to church regularly. I attended Born Again Church, the same church my parents brought us up in, and are presently serving at today. I was growing in the Lord and absorbing everything. I was in my mid-twenties and very zealous. About this time, I met a good friend to this day, Brother

Sean. Sean challenged me to do more than just come to church; he encouraged me to serve by joining the usher board. This was huge for me. I jumped in, hook, line, and sinker. I loved to serve. That is when I started wanting to do more for the Lord.

From there, ministry became a way of life. I went from serving on the usher board to helping lead the singles ministry. I then put together a mentoring program for young men called My Brother's Keeper. At that time, there was already a mentoring program for young ladies, called My Sister's Keeper, which was led by CeCe Winans and Demetrus Alexander. One day, Demetrus asked me if I ever thought about doing something for the boys. I prayed about it and talked to a few guys, and that is how My Brother's Keeper began.

I mentioned Demetrus because along with angels, there will be people who throw seeds out there to guide you along your journey. Sowers are like angels; the seeds they drop can come at the right time and launch, birth, and even ignite something in you that can set you on a course. When she asked me to consider putting together something for guys, it jump-started me towards my purpose.

By that time, I recognized that I always had the gift of

leadership, but now I wanted to use it for good. Since that moment, I have worked in several capacities to assist youth, men and boys from all walks of life, in Boys and Girls Club, Passport to Manhood, Woodland Hills Juvenile Detention Center, Franktown Open Hearts, My Friend's House, and Aphesis House. Currently, I serve as director of a YMCA program called Y-CAP (Community Action Project). We work with at-risk youth from Williamson County Juvenile Court and Alternative Learning Center and other kids from the community.

During those years, we also started a business called G3 Productions (G3 stands for Giving God Glory). Our company was a Christian entertainment firm. Those were phenomenal times. My birthday was on Halloween, and we would always host '70s parties. Those parties were so much fun and became so popular that we figured we should do it more than once a year. That is how the concept came to life. We ran with it from there.

Sean loved Holy Hip Hop and went on to become a DJ. We did everything from game parties, to bowling, to parties on the lake etc. G3 Productions became a ministry that kept a lot of singles from being bored with Christianity and allowed them to embrace and appreciate their single status. At that time, we were instrumental in making Christianity exciting for a lot of single and churches that did not have thriving single ministries.

I really felt the need to emphasize the power of a seed because the seeds we take in can also dictate where we will end up. At this point in my life, you could say I was on fire for God. He was speaking to me, and I was growing in grace daily. This was also when I met my future wife, Lovie.

Lovie's sister, Christyl, and I were involved in the singles ministry at Born Again Church. We were close friends, and she told me about her sister, who was moving to Nashville from Chicago. After Lovie moved here, we became very good friends. She and Christyl were two of the coolest girls I had ever hung out with. They loved sports, cooking, laughing, and having a good time with no drama. Four years later, I asked Lovie to marry me.

Now if you ask Lovie, she will say that four years was a long time. However, those four years were needed. I had a lot of growing up to do, especially if I wanted to marry someone of her caliber. At this stage, I was on the usher board, was president of My Brother's Keeper, and was running a Christian entertainment company, all at the same time. I thought I was hot stuff. You could not tell me nothing. I had become self-absorbed and was living on Pride Parkway, on the corner of Arrogance Boulevard.

The problem with that is that I had now fallen onto Righteous Ridge. This place can be just as harmful as Rebellion Ridge. The difference is, you cannot always see this one. This ridge is subtle and kind of sneaks up on you. That is the danger. Lovie moved to Nashville because she was going through a divorce. She was also the mother of a two-year-old daughter named Marlena. I never wanted to marry anyone who had children or had been divorced. That was my preference because I had never experienced either. God dealt with me harshly. I mean, He broke me down big time. I ended up losing my car, my apartment, my job, and my hustle. I was back in the Brokenness District again. The Bible says pride comes before destruction. Everything crumbled.

It's amazing how once you are broken, you begin to see things so clearly. You can also hear the still voice of God and humble yourself to obey as well. That's when God began to show me my ugly self.

He asked me, "If you could have babies, how many would you have?" He showed me how Lovie's divorce was not her fault and said, "How dare you judge her" knowing all I have forgiven you for. I was in no position to judge whatsoever. I remember telling a longtime friend who is now a pastor that I was saved.

His reply was, "No way, Les. You were worse than Paul."

While his words stung, I understood where he was coming from. This friend knows stuff that I cannot even put in this book. He knows me for real. How dare I hold anything against anyone? I have to say that marrying Lovie was the best thing that happened to me since turning my life over to the Lord. We have a lifetime of stories and miracles we can share from our nineteen years of marriage. Maybe we'll write a book together one day, if I ever get through with this one.

Those years after I came into the church, up to when I took on a wife, were some of the most formative and foundational years of my Christian development. I learned a lot and really got myself together. You know when you first get saved and everything is perfect, as you look out of your rose-colored glasses. You think everyone is blessed and highly favored and doing the right thing. You really think people have your best interest at heart, but then reality kicks in.

❓ REFLECTION QUESTIONS

What sowers and angels have shaped the course of your journey?

Who are the people God put in your life, and how have they changed your course?

What divine connections are you still bearing fruit from today?

If God hadn't sent you that angel, how would your life be different today?

CHAPTER 6

CROSSROADS

I HOPE THAT YOU ARE BEGINNING TO RECOGNIZE A pattern within this story. By the time you get through reading this, you should be able to identify and utilize this language to chart your own journey. You will continue to hear about hills and streets and districts and communities that you will be able to use as you design you own personal map to share your personal testimony. This will also raise your level of consciousness to keep you away from these dangerous areas that could take you off course, as you pursue your purpose.

If this was a TV show, this time would be considered a commercial break. If you are still reading, you have already heard about the first half of my life. I want to pause here because I, like many others, was one of those who thought that since I gave my life over to the Lord, everything would be great. That's just not realistic. There are still so many things to learn about God and yourself and others. It's really a never-ending class. Once you get one thing down, God will show you another area. It ends up being good stuff, but when you are in it, it doesn't always feel good. It can be quite humbling.

When I look back over the second half of my life, I realize how much I did not know in the first half. I thought that I was ahead of the curve. In hindsight, I can see how dumb a lot of my decisions were. Let us take a praise break. The name of this break is "Amazing Grace." This grace I am talking about kept me when I did not want to keep myself. In life, you come to places where you must make a choice. On your map, these will be called crossroads. Some of these crossroads can mean life or death, or take you completely off course.

I made many bone-headed decisions over my life that easily could have hurt my future or cost me my life. There have been several times that I was guilty, like the time a friend and I got caught getting high at Centennial Park. We were both handcuffed and taken downtown to night court. My friend ended up taking full responsibility for the drugs. I was released, and he went to jail. If he had not said the drugs were his, we both would have been booked, and I would not be able to work many of the jobs I've worked because I would have been a felon. The truth of the matter is, we went in half on the drugs, and I should have been charged.

That's just one of the times I have been spared. Before I got married, I remember literally holding my breath during a pregnancy test. The young lady taking the test and I both knew that I had no plans to marry her. How would my life have been different if the test came back positive? Would I have been a good father? Would I have married her just to try to do the right thing? Would I have walked away? I have no idea, but God said not guilty, even though I was guilty. I was wrong, but God's grace did not sentence me in that situation.

I've been held at gunpoint by bounty hunters who were looking for a friend, who was a big-time dope dealer. I think they were bounty hunters; that's what they said. All I know is, they came into his house, pointed their guns at us, and made us all get on the ground (even his mom). They searched the whole house. When they could not find what they were looking for, they ran out the back door. What if he had been there? What if they had killed everyone and took the dope? I know that happens because that is what happened to the bully from middle school:

robbed and killed. God had my back again and got me out of another bad situation.

I could share many things that could have altered my life forever, but we're trying to go somewhere. In a snapshot, I have been in fights and arguments that could have easily gone very bad, and I could have been killed. I have been in car wrecks that I should not have walked away from, not to mention being behind the wheel while high or drunk that I don't even know how I got home. All of this is to say that the choices you make will alter your course, and some cannot be repaired. As you look back over your journey, reflect on how God's amazing grace has kept you on course.

❓ REFLECTION QUESTIONS

What turns would you change if you could?

What wrong directions have you contributed to the lives of others?

Are you at a crossroad in your life now?

Do you know about this amazing grace that I'm talking about?

CHAPTER 7

CHURCH FOLK

PUT ON YOUR SEATBELT BECAUSE THIS IS WHERE IT gets tricky. As I shared, the years after I came into the church were some of the best years of my life. What I did not share is how this is also where you can get hurt by people you encounter while attending. My brothers and sisters, let me tell you that there is no hurt like church hurt. Let the church say amen. I had to say it. I feel this is the worst kind of hurt because it usually come from people you think know the Lord or even helped you somewhere along the line in your walk. Also, how do you cope when the place you went to for healing hurts you? People refer to the church as a spiritual hospital. Imagine going to the doctor for a checkup and catching COVID-19? What then?

This is where I experienced a huge learning curve.

One of the many lessons I learned is to not put confidence in other people or in your own flesh. This is scriptural. When I started doing better and felt that I was on the right track, a subtle enemy snuck his way in: pride. These devils are prevalent, especially in the church. You see, when I was over the various ministries, I thought I had it going on. I started to think I was really doing something because I was serving. I also began to look down on people who were not doing as much as I was. I had fallen in a state of self-righteousness and did not even know it. This is a class that you can take at church or in life, and not even know you are in it.

On my map, this place is called Righteousness Ridge. Righteous Ridge is a whole group of hills and mountains that are just as dangerous as Rebellion Ridge. The problem with these mountains is that you think you are doing everything right; you become prideful and begin to judge others. On Righteous Ridge, you will find all kinds of traps like pride, envy, self-righteousness, covetousness, jealousy, slothfulness, greed, deceit, gossip, judging, selfishness, boasting, complaining, strife, contention, laziness, wrong motives, idolatry, lust, gluttony, fornication, preferential treatment, and the list goes on. I could go on for days with the traps that you could find yourself in.

When I finally got married, I felt that the Lord wanted me to leave my home church and begin our new journey as Mr. and Mrs. Lester. I found out that if you are building the kingdom following the blueprint of leadership, it is okay. Even if you see unstable structures, gaping holes, or faulty materials in the plan, you should remain silent and not speak up, if it's the church house. I know couples who have had huge fights and even divorced because one spouse was more committed to the church than the marriage. In a lot of cases, once you begin to look out for what is best for you and your family, you can be considered as out of order and even walking in rebellion, unfaithful to the vision of the church (or "Man of God").

At one church, the minister asked Lovie and I to oversee their youth ministry. While we had our reservations, we were humbled and excited to serve. We loved everything about the ministry; we just did not like the way they treated the previous youth minister. We should have seen this as a red flag, but we wanted to help. At the time, our daughter was in the youth ministry, which motivated us even more to serve. We served faithfully for a year. Lovie was writing curriculum, planning, scheduling, and teaching. All this while working full-time as a teacher and caring for our two children. At this time, Sam, our son, began to have some health concerns. We decided she needed to step down because it was too taxing on our family.

I called the office and requested a meeting with the pastor. Two weeks later, no one had reached out; I was told that he was busy. Since I was unable to get on the calendar, I decided to tell him during our weekly staff meeting. When it was time for me to give my update at the staff meeting, I explained that Lovie had not been feeling well, and we were concerned about my son and the health challenges he was having. You see Sam (our miracle son) was born three months prematurely. He was born weighing one pound, fourteen ounces. He was around two years old at the time, so we were just beginning our journey with him and noticing he was not meeting the milestones of his typical peers.

After I shared all of this, his replied, "Are you finished?" I said yes. He next said, "You don't leave holes in my ministry. Don't come and tell me that your wife is stepping down. You bring me her replacement. You're new, but everyone here knows how I run my ministry."

My reply was, "Yes, I am new, and that is why I wanted to meet with you prior to this meeting."

He replied, "There's no reason to meet because you're fired."

This was the day I discovered I was saved for real. In my previous life, I would have gladly gone to jail that day. You know I had a fighting spirit on me. Something kept me from losing it. Till this day, I am still baffled that I didn't respond like I had done several times before. Maybe because God had started putting me on a different course.

This is where we as Christians, in many cases, can fumble the ball. I have done this, and I could again, if I'm not careful and prayerful. I also know Christians who have lied to me and disappointed me in other instances. At one point, Lovie and I took a three-year sabbatical from church because we had been wounded on the battlefield.

Okay, I'll give you one more example. I have a creative side. Over my lifetime, I have started several different ventures; some were before Christ, like So Phi, Totally Ruthless & Unique MF Posse (TRUMP: do not ask), Watch Me, and Blackberries. After I gave my life to the Lord, I started Christian entrepreneurial ventures like G3, Calvary Clothing, Kinfolk, and our nonprofit, Servants of the Lord Disciplined in Excellence, Righteousness, and Submission (SOLDIERS) International.

Before we launched Calvary Clothing in 2003, I had an idea for a Christian business model. I pulled together eight of the strongest Christian men I knew and shared my idea with them. Some were elders or leaders at the church. It was called Kingdom Investment Network (KIN). I proposed that we all put in a certain amount of money (I think it was about four hundred dollars), and we would look for investment opportunities to put our money into. In about two months, our money had tripled.

It just so happened that two of the brothers were in the car business, and one had a car lot. These two got together and pulled a couple of others in and convinced them to buy one of the cars off the lot to give to a single mom. They called an emergency meeting, but no one could attend. We had established a rule that decisions required a quorum of at least four members. Now here I was, one of four to attend this meeting. The other three already had their minds set on this investment. The problem I had was that it was going to take almost all the money invested.

I also had a problem with it because it was for a single mom, and the cars the guys were selling were not reliable. I think he had a total of four cars at best. What if the car broke down and the single mom's investment was gone? How would we look in the eyes of our fellow brothers and sisters if the deal went bad? I recommended that we wait till more members could come before we took a vote. They said that we had a quorum, and I could not change the rules. My dad was one of the eight who were unable to attend. He knew that I was upset and asked to meet with the guys.

When we met, they told him that a vote had been taken, and if I didn't like it, they were going to kick me out. These Christian brothers also said that I could not get my money back because it was already decided on.

Now let us look at this. I am getting strong-armed out of the group I put together, and they're going to take my money? Keep in mind, I had the utmost respect for these guys before this happened. Money and greed turned them into something else. The sad thing is that we had not even made any substantial monetary gains.

Then one brother in the group said, "We can't do Lamont like this. This was his vision."

They ended up putting me out of the group but gave me my money back. My dad left the group soon after, and then the investment network folded. I was so glad that I had gotten out of that group because shortly thereafter, God gave me the vision for a Christian clothing line called Kinfolk.

To bring it home, Righteousness Ridge brought me to Disappointment Drive and eventually landed me in the Bitterness District. I lived there for at least five years, upset with church folk and self-righteous leaders who had made themselves gods. I distinctly remember not going to church on Sundays and watching TBN or trying to find a comforting pastor to listen to. Thank God for Pastor Hannah at New Life Southeast in Chicago. We still follow his ministry.

These are things you do not see coming when you're wearing rose-colored glasses. They can blindside you and knock you completely off course. The sad thing is, most of these people are Christians and love the Lord. Either way, when people have been hurt by Christians in church, the impact can be devastating, and you can travel on Healing Highway for a long time, waiting for a sturdy off-ramp.

❓ REFLECTION QUESTIONS

Have you or anyone you know ever experienced Church Hurt?

How do you think today's society is dealing with this?

Have you ever gotten caught in one of the traps on Righteous Ridge?

Who let you down and made you visit Disappointment Drive?

CHAPTER 8

ON THE ROAD AGAIN

Healing Highway is the road that you want to be on. It is inevitable that you will encounter some bumps and bruises and even some wrong turns. When these things happen, it is imperative that you make your way back to this road. There are some streets, neighborhoods, and communities that you don't want to hang out in.

After leaving the Bitterness District and working through my hurtful church experiences, I got back into another local church. By then, we had also started our Christian clothing line. The first line we introduced was called Kinfolk, which was created to break down racial and denominational barriers that keep us separated. Kinfolk was based on Genesis 12:1-3, which talks about Abraham and his seed. Kinfolk are people who share common ancestry, family, relatives, or kin. Simply stated, descendants of Abraham's seed are kinfolk through the blood line of Jesus Christ.

I personally had no background with design and knew nothing about the clothing business. I had a concept, and the Lord put in my path a young man named Terry who could design shirts. I told him about my idea, and he went to work. He designed four baseball jerseys (which were very popular back in the day), and the rest was history. We were selling jerseys and hats and eventually a full line for kids and women. You could not tell me that this wasn't from God. We eventually worked our way up to two locations. We had a bookstore in our church called the Glory Spot and a Calvary Clothing kiosk in the mall.

Just when you think things are beginning to look up, life happens. Lovie and I had been praying to God for years for a second child, and suddenly, we had a baby coming. We had lost a child once through miscarriage and were very concerned because of Lovie's age. Our newborn baby came three months early, and then the economy crashed. Yes, I did say that our son was born three months early. Our prayers were answered and on August 17th, our son Sam entered the world. Now, a premature son brings on a concerns and fears, now I was on the cusp of having a newborn son. Now I was on the cusp of having my first biological child and having a son of my own.

The miracle of Samuel's birth is a story within itself. As a matter of fact, my mother has been instrumental in helping women write their stories, and Lovie shared Sam's story in one of her books, *Memories of Faith*. Sam's existence has done nothing but increase our faith by giving us the opportunity to live with a miracle. Some people do not believe in miracles, and others don't think they still happen. For fourteen years, we've seen the hand of God on Sam's life, and it's been nothing short of miraculous. If you ask Lovie, she'll say that Samuel's birth changed me. I am not sure what that means, so you'll have to ask her about that. I just know that I have found myself waiting for God to show up in so many ways. He is faithful and does just that. His plan continues to unfold right before my very eyes, to the point that we are probably going to have to write a book about it as well, because if I told you, you would not believe it.

Since we need to continue this journey, I will get back on track. It was a discouraging experience when the economy crashed; we had to close our stores down. A friend of mine, Gary, knew I had the clothing line and got me on at K&G, a new department store in Nashville.

I ended up managing the suit department there for about six years. I often wondered how I ended back up on the sales floor. I questioned everything God was doing, from my son coming early to having a business that failed. I remember feeling as if the Lord was asking me, "Have you had to give up something you really loved? Do you love Me more?" I remember surrendering and just accepting what the Lord was doing.

Although I was on my way to healing, I had to travel on this long strip called Patience Parkway. Now, this street is a beast. I really feel like the Lord had me on this road forever; in fact, I am still on it. The book of James talks about patience having "her" perfect work. This perfect work can be extremely frustrating, to say the least. By the time I had gotten to Nordstrom, I was in my tenth straight year of retail and really did not see a way out. You must remember that I didn't have a degree and didn't want to go back to school. The economy tanked, and we needed the double insurance coverage from my job to be on the safe side for Sam.

While working at Nordstrom one day, I met two guys from Africa. I had moved my way up to become a personal stylist, which gave me a higher percentage on all my sales. As a matter of fact, I was doing very well. The two guys asked if we could have coffee one day. They were believers, so I agreed. Sitting upstairs at the Starbucks in Green Hills, they asked if they could pray for me, and of course I said yes. They began to prophecy about the calling that was on my life and what was to come.

I must take a minute here to say that I am convinced that prophecies are love letters from God. There have been several times when I've been at a crossroad, and God sent someone to tell me what "thus says the Lord." This was one of those times. The men prophesied that God was going to uproot me and plant me in a place where I would grow like never before. They also said I would have favor there and would be able to walk in my purpose. They mentioned that my roots would go deep, and the Lord would bless me in this place. They said the position was made for me, and I would flourish.

This was not the first time this had happened. God knows when to send a love letter, just like we would if we had a spouse or someone we loved. For example, the Lord dropped me a love letter years before I met Lovie. That prophecy disclosed several of her characteristics and explained how she would carry herself and the effect she would have on me. I held on to it and did not budge until I met her several years later. I mention that to show that there are lions and other evil forces looking to get you off track, but God, Who is rich in mercy, also has angels and seeds and love letters out there to get you where you need to be.

After a few months passed by, an old friend from K&G came in and said he had been looking for me. He asked me if I was still interested in working with kids. Of course, I said yes. He asked if I wanted to work with inner city kids in Franklin, Tennessee. I responded that Franklin didn't really have an inner city, but I took the job, which was with a nonprofit called Franktown Open Hearts. FTOH worked with lower income families (99 percent African American). I started working with these kids and their families, and absolutely loved it. I've been doing this work for the past twenty years. Life was good. I had escaped retail and was finally doing the work I loved.

??? REFLECTION QUESTIONS

What happens when "suddenly" all your plans fail?

Have you found yourself attempting to fix everything again?

Is the Lord using Patience Parkway to work something out in you?

"Have you had to give up something you really loved?"

CHAPTER 9

THE FINAL TEST

They say that hindsight is 20/20. As I look back at fifty years old, I really feel there was a plan all along. COVID-19 changed the way we do things, and now everything is different. I still work with young people, but I've had to adapt to virtual platforms because we can no longer get together in large groups. I had some youth in my program attend an online workshop on perseverance. Most of my kids were dealing with something, but one young lady said she had never experienced anything that took her breath away. We were discussing George Floyd and talking about when life knocks the wind out of you. It was a good discussion. I did tell her that if it hasn't happened yet, it will probably happen sometime in her lifetime.

    I only mention this because I ended the last chapter

with "Life was good." It was good, but there is always that "to be continued. ..." My to-be-continued looked like me in my new position working with kids, churches, and the community: a dream come true. I think Job 30:26 says it best: "When I looked for good, then evil came."

A new lion entered. I once had a close friend become my supervisor and he began to micromanage and criticize everything I did. We started off as a good team and did great for the first year. After that, something changed. I am not sure what it was, but I really began to feel like I was on the defensive every day, about everything. I remember feeling like David when Saul began to treat him a certain way. Didn't Saul ask for David to come? Didn't my friend say he had been looking for me to come and help him in Franklin? Why did I keep feeling spears fly past my head? Another woman who worked there also felt the heat. She quit because she could not take it anymore.

About two years in, I was extremely frustrated with the work environment, and one day, it came to a tipping point. My supervisor and I discussed one of the kids in our program. He felt that I did not handle the situation right, which seemed like it happened every hour, and I just told him I could not work in that environment anymore. At that point, we had a heated exchange. Now mind you, I am a fighter and loved to fight in my previous life. Something in me held me back and made me ask, "What are we doing?" I talked to him about what it would look like for two African American men, who were supposed to be helping young people cope, ruin the program for everyone because we could not get along.

There were only two things that could happen when things get to a boiling point: one person gets hurt badly, and the other goes to jail. From my experience, that is the only conclusion I saw. This was the second time in my life where I said to myself that I was saved for real. No one had messed with me since the eighth grade without paying a price for it. It must be Jesus. Hindsight being 20/20, I think of what fighting and being a hot head had cost me when I worked at Target years ago. God brought me back to the same test, and He will bring you back as well, if you do not pass. This time, I passed.

My supervisor decided to resign and move on, but I did not want his position because I did not want it to look like I took his job. Therefore, I stayed in my position, and the organization hired a new director. Sadly, this was not a good fit, either. It seemed like the more I did to assist our church and the organization, the more the new supervisor questioned my commitment. One day, he said that it looked like I had too many things on my plate, and he was concerned about my focus.

Where he got that from, I do not know. He clearly did not understand the structure and vision I had helped create prior to his arrival. We shaped that program and laid a super foundation for anyone who would come behind us. We also did not agree on how to impact the community we served. Ironically, today (post-George Floyd), we are in a place where there have been several discussions about systemic racism and white supremacy. These discussions speak to the underlining pride some white people can have (white privilege), which makes them feel that they are right. These discussions point out that some people completely discount black and brown voices. I am not saying that this is the case here, but I felt as if my voice was not appreciated, and I was forced to resign.

The thing that hurt about that situation was that I had formed several relationships with the families and churches in the community. The kids I had been working with were used to people walking out of their lives. They had grown accustomed to a lack of consistency. I had been an intricate part of helping our home church with initial conversations about racial reconciliation. In the midst, it felt like my new supervisor (who happened to be white) discounted me and my work. It took some time for me to see that even this situation was all a part of God's plan. His ways are definitely not our ways, but it's all good.

Once again, I moved back into the Brokenness District and stayed for several months. I did a lot of reflecting and wondering how I got back to this wilderness space again. It did not help that I was working the graveyard shift (10 p.m. to 6 a.m.) at Nissan, making car seats. It was confusing because I felt that I had done things right but had gotten the short end of the stick. I remembered how things were so good when I first arrived and thought I had finally found something tailor-made for me. How did it end so terribly? It was a challenging six months.

One day, Lovie, Sam, and I decided to go for a drive to visit Franklin. We rode through the community and talked about some of the good times I had experienced while working there. While driving, a few of the kids I had worked with came running toward my car. I ended up stopping, and more kids started running up, saying, "Hey, it's Mr. Lamont!" So many kids came up to us and expressed how much they missed me; they all asked why I left them. We were completely overwhelmed. The love we were shown that day convinced me there was still work for me to do in Franklin. When I talk about life knocking the breath out of you, my abrupt departure from Franklin had done just that.

From there, Lovie and I went into prayer. When we need answers and direction, that is what we do because it works. Our prayer was for God to confirm for us that He started the work in Franklin for me, and He wanted me to finish it. If it was so, we asked God to open that door. I also had to drink the healing waters found at Forgiveness Fountain. We were praying for something to happen, but we could not see how God would do it. The only thing we knew for sure was that holding on to bitterness was not going to move God toward us and our situation.

Around that time, a position at the YMCA Williamson County Y-CAP opened for a summer program. I knew the director because the program I left and his program were both housed in the same building. I ended up leaving Nissan and taking this part-time position (which paid a fraction of what I was making) for the summer. The first week I was there, the director said, "I think some blessings are coming your way". Although we had talked many times over the years, we rarely discussed godly principles. But I received what he said anyway. After working there for just three weeks, he informed me that he was leaving the program. I came in as the assistant coordinator, with another person over me. By the time the summer ended, I had been asked to interview for the program head, and the Lord blessed me to be hired as the director of the program.

I became the director of the YMCA Community Action Project (Y-CAP), an afterschool and summer program for at-risk teens. My job is to build relationships in the community that benefit young people in Williamson County. We partner with Juvenile Court, the Alternative Learning Center, Williamson County Schools, the Beat of Life, My Friend's House, the Refuge Counseling Center, and various other nonprofit organizations. I am also the staff lead with the Spirit/Mind committee for the Brentwood YMCA of Middle Tennessee and a part of the Diversity and Inclusion Group (DIG) committee.

Our YCAP programs are held in the same place I was working before. Only now, we have access to the entire space, which has been reimaged with the help of the students we serve. The students wanted a music room and prayer/meditation room. We designed everything to fit their needs. I am finally in the place where every gift and talent I have can be fully utilized. However, I am no longer naïve. I know that the enemy is waiting in the cut, but I've also learned that the Lord will never leave me nor forsake me. I know that all things work out for my good because I am called according to His purpose. I also know that the Lord had a plan all along, and I am just on a journey to my purpose place.

⁇ REFLECTION QUESTIONS

Which tests do you continue to retake?

What test are you passing?

Are you ready for your final exam to graduate into purpose?

Who are the people you are supposed to go back and get?

CHAPTER 10

IN PURPOSE, ON PURPOSE

Purpose Place is where the Lord took the culmination of my experiences and allowed me to utilize them now. During these peaks and valleys, we started our own nonprofit called Servants of the Lord Disciplined in Excellence, Righteousness, and Submission (SOLDIERS) International. We also partner with churches and communities in Nashville and the surrounding counties to facilitate discussions and host listening circles on topics related to racial reconciliation. This is done specifically through the Harmony CORE-alition group.

My experiences have brought me to a place where I can honestly say there are not many people who are more equipped to share real-life experiences and make them applicable to your situation. I have read, studied, and executed several mentoring programs over the years. This one is unique in that it is completely adaptive. It is applicable to your situation because it takes your journey and helps you makes sense of it. Now you are probably wondering, what mentoring program? I am glad you asked. You have just been introduced to MAP's Mentoring Module. This module will equip you to do exactly what I just did to get you unstuck. Once you are free, you are equipped to help someone else get unstuck.

I also have to say that you should attend the workshop to fully apply what you just read. Your MAP will show you where you are and help you chart the course for your next destination.

Congratulations. You have completed the first phase, and I hope that it was insightful. From here, I would recommend you begin to look back over your life and answer these questions using some of the language you have read about (Shame Street, Healing Highway, Anger Alley, and so on):

- Where are you now?
- How did you get there?
- When did you encounter your first lion?
- How did you get off course?

- Have you ever confronted a lion in your life?
- Have you ever visited Shame Street?
- Have you been to the Brokenness District?
- What seeds have shaped the course of your journey?
- Who are the people God put in your life who have changed your course?
- What divine connections are you still bearing fruit from today?
- What right or wrong turns have you made on your course?
- What turns would you change if you could?
- What wrong directions have you contributed in other lives?
- Are you at a crossroads in your life now?
- Is the Lord using Patience Parkway to work something out in you?

There are many other communities and streets that I would love to tell you about. Some I have visited, others I know about from people who have visited and shared their postcards. One of the most common neighborhoods men visit is Denial Drive. Have you ever been on that street? I have. It's another place I've visited on my journey. My goal is to give you a snapshot of what you will experience while making your personal map.

In conclusion, I would do you a serious disservice if I did not share with you why it is so important to get to Purpose Place, where you realize all your experiences and stops along your journey were strategically designed for you to help someone else. What we do not realize on our journey is, there are people the Lord has assigned to help you get to your purpose. Once there, you are to assist others on their journey to purpose. What I am currently experiencing is so much bigger than me. Sounds churchy, but let me explain.

I arrived at my purpose by seeking the Lord for the plan He had for my life. Once it was revealed, I had to be patient and wait for Him to send people who shared the same heart and spirit for the Kingdom as me. I know I cannot accomplish what He wants me to do alone. These people have gifts and levels of expertise I do not have. Together, we are working diligently to accomplish the plan. Our goal is to bring glory to Him in whatever we accomplish.

While in purpose, I have gained the necessary tools to go back into my MAP and journey, and help people who have walked similar paths as mine. I hope to share escape routes and wisdom. In my story, you read of the several traps and strongholds I had to work through. I wish I could tell you I am a great escape artist. However, in hindsight, I know it was only the grace and mercy of the Lord that kept me alive.

Thank you for taking the time to read about this new language. I am confident it will assist people from all walks of life to chart their course and share their story. These days, so many people are determined to be something else. It is important we remove our masks and show the world our authentic selves. Who God has created you to be is significant, and your story is vital. I pray this has inspired you enough to roll up your sleeves and begin the journey and create your community. I look forward to seeing you in one of our workshops. We would be honored to help you map out your journey and usher you into your place of purpose.

PART 2

AN INTRODUCTION TO MAP LANGUAGE THERAPY

MAP is a curriculum-based program designed to help people navigate through the everyday challenges, barriers, and traps they face in their life. MAP is comprised of keys, tips, and pointers that will educate and empower people to avoid these traps and get out of those they are caught up in. These keys are laid out in a curriculum broken down into workshops or teaching sessions that share strategies to assist individuals on their journey.

MAP will take you on an adventure, looking for the one treasure that can help you in your life. The key to successfully finishing your course depends on your ability to find the treasure.

One workshop example is "Who's Shaping Your Course?" This workshop teaches individuals that their life is a journey, and they are supposed to be going somewhere.

On this road, there are going to be forces (both good and bad) pulling on them. This session helps people identify influences that have shaped them and their thinking. By the end of the course, they should be able to identify the negative and positive influences in their lives and make informed decisions which put them on the plan designed for them.

MAP is an adventure comprised of streets, hills, mountains, neighborhoods, and communities that tell about the journey most people travel. This map will also allow them to chart their own courses and avoid pitfalls and dangers. To better assist you in implementing our model, let me tell you about some of the areas you will be learning about:

Rebellion Ridge is an area that is full of trees and traps that are hard to get through. Some of these hills can take days, months, and even years to navigate through. The people who stay the longest, do not heed advice or receive wise counsel from anyone. They feel they are right in their decisions, but the evidence of their choices proves that is not the case! Unfortunately, some people do not make it through. Some even die stuck in the wilderness.

Anger Alley is often traveled and does not have many off-ramps attached to it. In most cases, this alley is visited by people who have been hurt or offended. It can be a short walk, but some people stay there for long periods of time, although it was made to pass through.

Disappointment District is a community where people who have gotten down on their luck reside; they do not know how to get back up again and feel desperate and hopeless. Be careful not to walk too far on this road because it can lead to Depression Avenue.

Bitterness Block is another place you do not want to go. The people there generally are not friendly. In their minds, they have been burned, and they spent so much time in Anger Alley, they cannot forgive. You often see them lashing out at other people because they have been hurt. I think this is where the phrase "Hurt people, hurt people" originated. This is a bad neighborhood.

Broken District is unique and distinct. This is where a lot of people come to their senses and get on the right track. They are open to wisdom and reasoning they would not listen to before. Although this place can lead you to the right track, some people do not heed the lessons and must go back.

Escape Parkway is a road given with every temptation and allows you to get away from the lions. In every situation, there is an escape door. Too often, we do not take advantage of it and end up in places we are not supposed to be in. Some off-ramps have big signs, but others are more subtle, so it's important to be observant on your journey. When you miss the sign, your whole life can change, with lasting effects. Please keep an eye out for the escape signs because your life and your future could depend on it.

Healing Highway has a beautiful drive. On it, you will see things you have never seen before. You will begin to look at people and situations with clarity. It's a peaceful ride; usually, you'll do more listening than talking. The views and scenery are awesome. One of the favorite stops is Forgiveness Fountain. People from all over the world drink from this fountain and are instantly set free to continue their journey in peace and love. I have personally had to travel this road many times.

Patience Parkway is a looooooong road that most people do not like to use. Unlike Healing Highway, the scenery and views are not nice at all. In fact, it can be a rough ride, with potholes and poor lighting. It is not as quick, but you learn so much more on this road. It also has everything you need to make you whole and complete for your journey. The downside is that the off-ramps may have several people in front of you because the lines are long. Nevertheless, if you can make it down this road, it is rewarding and will make your future trips a lot easier.

Shame Street is lonely. You rarely see a lot of people hanging out together. In most cases, this is where you must live with yourself after making a mistake or bad decision. People stay longer if the mistake was public. It is generally quiet, to encourage self-reflection. Be careful not to stay there long because it is the gateway to other neighborhoods that are much worse.

Depression Avenue is not where you want to be. These dark streets have been known to trap people for years. That is not the worse part. It leads to so many other lonely communities, including one of the worst neighborhoods, Suicide Circle. Be careful. You may not come back from there. People are dying daily. Keep out.

Self-Pity Pike is where the blame game was created. A lot of people on this street see themselves as victims, and few of them take responsibility for their actions; they blame others for their shortcomings. It can be loud, and you always see someone pulled over, telling their version of what happened. If you listen closely, you will hear their conversations are generally laced with excuses of why things did not go as planned.

The Iso Islands are where people go when they do not want anyone around them. They are way off and far away from any land. This is also a place where the lions encourage you to visit because there is no one there to help you get back on track. A lot of people are very sick and even die out there because support, services, and resources are cut off. Whatever you do, stay the course, and don't visit these islands when you're discouraged because you may not come back.

Purpose Place is awesome. Can you say heaven on earth? This is where all your travels were designed to get you. This is where everything you learned on your journey comes together, and you use it as fuel to go back to the starting line and teach others how to avoid traps. This is when your travels and experience pay off because you are now a GPS for others, following in your footsteps. You help them navigate now. You realize that you have taken this whole journey just to start over and sit in the passenger seat and be a copilot for someone who is lost.

You will also see several things on your journey, such as the following:

Lions represent people or influences designed to get you off course. Lions take on many forms, but all have the same job description: steal, kill, and destroy.

Crossroad signs. You will run into these throughout your journey. These will help you in your decision making. Your journey can be a lot safer and more peaceful if you take the right route. They become very important as you move forward because unlike the lion that comes to get you off course, the crossroad signs allow you to get back on course.

Traps. There are several of these all over your journey. They are designed to trip you up and keep you there. The cool thing is that with every trap, there is a way of escape. You must become aware of the escape routes as you move forward. In a lot of cases, people are not defensive drivers and become easily distracted, which causes them to miss the exit signs. Consequently, they end up lost and often trapped because they fell asleep at the wheel.

Forgiveness Fountain. You will find this along the way as you drive on Patience Parkway and Healing Highway. This is a must-see attraction if you are planning on going to Purpose Place. Sometimes, if you do not stop by the fountain, they will not let you into Purpose Place. They usually make you go back to the neighborhood where you were hurt and deal with yourself. Once you do that, you are now validated to get into your purpose.

Angels are people, places, events, and things designed to get you back on the right path. As you go along in your journey, be cautious of your surroundings. Make sure you keep your ears and eyes open for things that are true, good, right, pure, lovely, or admirable. These mile markers are put in your path for a reason and will help you along the way.

- Look at these communities, neighborhoods, and streets, and see how many you can identify with.
- Begin to chart your own course or explore the option of teaching others how to use this tool.

When you MAP out your life and become who God created you to be, it paints a beautiful picture.

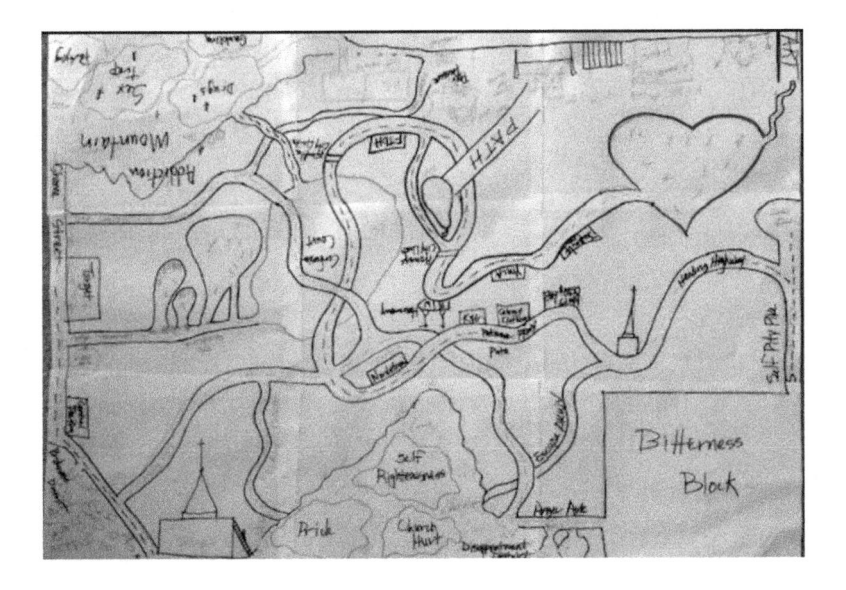